Wild Britain

Bat

Louise and Richard Spilsbury

Heinemann
LIBRARY

H www.heinemann.co.uk
Visit our website to find out more information about Heinemann Library books.

To order:
☎ Phone 44 (0) 1865 888066
📄 Send a fax to 44 (0) 1865 314091
💻 Visit the Heinemann Bookshop at www.heinemann.co.uk to browse our catalogue and order online.

First published in Great Britain by Heinemann Library, Halley Court, Jordan Hill, Oxford OX2 8EJ, part of Harcourt Education Ltd. Heinemann is a registered trademark of Harcourt Education Ltd.

Editorial: Lucy Thunder and Helen Cannons
Design: David Poole and Celia Floyd
Illustrations: Jeff Edwards, Alan Fraser and Geoff Ward
Picture Research: Rebecca Sodergren and Peter Morris
Production: Edward Moore

Originated by Repro Multi-Warna
Printed and bound in China by South China Printing Company

The paper used to print this book comes from sustainable resources.

ISBN 0 431 03985 2 (hardback)
08 07 06 05 04
10 9 8 7 6 5 4 3 2 1

ISBN 0 431 03992 5 (paperback)
09 08 07 06 05
10 9 8 7 6 5 4 3 2 1

British Library Cataloguing in Publication Data
Spilsbury, Louise and Spilsbury, Richard
Bat. – (Wild britain)
599.4'0941

A full catalogue record for this book is available from the British Library.

Acknowledgements

The Publishers would like to thank the following for permission to reproduce photographs:

Ardea/E. Mickleburgh p26; Bruce Coleman/Kim Taylor p6; Corbis/Joe McDonald p8; FLPA/B. Borrell pp5, 22; FLPA/B. S. Turner p15; FLPA/D'Accunto/Panda p24; FLPA/David Hosking p16; FLPA/H Clark pp18, 20, 23; NHPA/Stephen Dalton pp10, 11, 14; NHPA/Melvin Grey pp4, 21, 28; NHPA/Michael Leach p27; NPL/Duncan McEwan p17; Oxford Scientific Films pp12, 13; Oxford Scientific Films/Tony Tilford p19; Oxford Scientific Films/Richard Packwood pp9, 29; Woodfall Wild Images/Steve Austin p25.

Cover photograph of a pipistrelle bat flying at night, reproduced with permission of NHPA/Stephen Dalton.

The Publishers would like to thank Michael Scott for his assistance in the preparation of this book.

Every effort has been made to contact copyright holders of any material reproduced in this book. Any omissions will be rectified in subsequent printings if notice is given to the Publisher.

Contents

Any words appearing in the text in bold, **like this**, are explained in the Glossary.

What are bats?

Whiskered bats, like this one, live in woodlands.

Bats are the only **mammals** that can fly. .
Bats have leathery wings, furry bodies and
large ears. There are sixteen different kinds
of bats that live in Britain.

A pipistrelle bat weighs around the same as a one pound coin. Its body is about the size of an adult's thumb.

Pipistrelle bats are the most common bats in Britain. They are also the smallest. They are dark brown with a light brown belly. Their ears are shaped like triangles.

Where do bats live?

If you see bats around trees in a town or city, they are most likely to be pipistrelle bats.

Pipistrelle bats live along hedgerows and around **marshes**, woodland and farmland. They also live in gardens and parks in towns and cities.

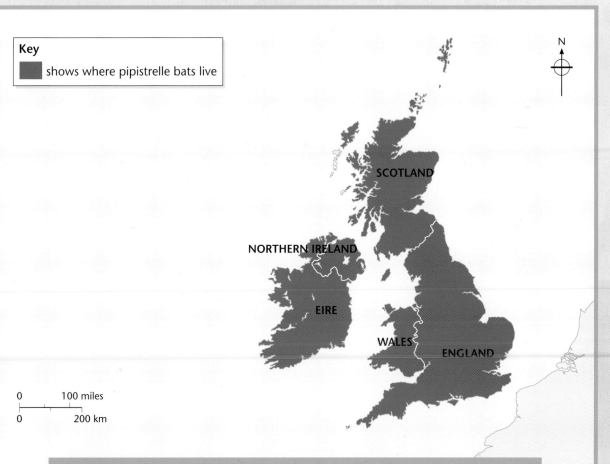

Key

shows where pipistrelle bats live

SCOTLAND

NORTHERN IRELAND

EIRE

WALES

ENGLAND

0   100 miles

0   200 km

This map shows that pipistrelle bats are found in most parts of Britain and Ireland.

Bats do not usually live in wide-open spaces. They live in places where there are trees, houses or other sheltered places to hide in.

What do bats eat?

A pipistrelle bat may eat more than 3000 insects in one night!

Bats are **nocturnal** animals. That means that they come out at night to find food. Pipistrelle bats **hunt** and eat **insects**, such as flies, moths and midges.

Bats have sharp pointed teeth to hold and crunch their food.

Bats catch small insects in their mouths. They usually eat their food while they are flying. Bats may eat larger insects on a **perch,** such as a branch or rooftop.

Finding food

Bats hunt in the dark when it is hard to see. They use sounds to find their food.

Bats find food using **echolocation**. They make high squeaks that we cannot hear. When the sounds hit something, the **echoes** bounce back to the bat.

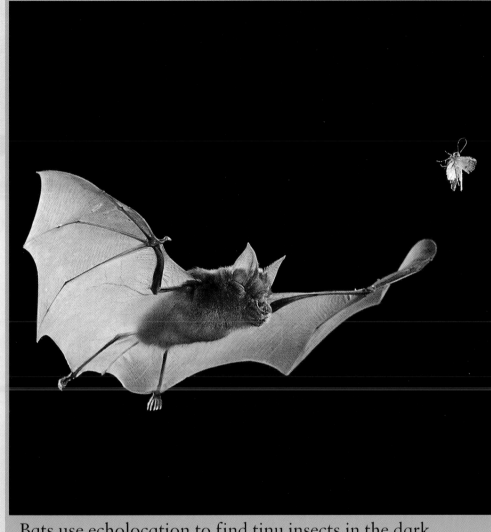

Bats use echolocation to find tiny insects in the dark.

A bat listens to the echoes from its squeaks. It uses the echoes to work out where an **insect** is. Then the bat swoops in and catches it.

On the move

Pipistrelle bats can twist and dive quickly in the air.
They hardly ever land on the ground.

Pipistrelle bats fly in a fast, jerky way.
They dodge about trying to catch **insects** in
the air. They use **echolocation** to avoid
bumping into trees and other obstacles.

Can you see the bones in this greater horseshoe bat's wings?

Inside a bat's wing there are five very long fingers of bone, like a hand. There is a thin skin over and between the bones. This makes the wing.

Resting and sleeping

Bats sleep somewhere high up, out of reach of animals that try to eat them.

Bats use up a lot of **energy** flying fast between dusk and dawn. They rest and sleep during the day. Bats mostly sleep hanging upside down.

The claws on a bat's feet hold it tightly on to a perch.

Bats have five sharp claws on each foot. The claws grip on to their **perch**. The weight of their body makes the claws lock into place. This stops them from falling off.

Bat groups

This group of long-eared bats is resting in an attic.

Bats usually get together in groups to rest and sleep. Up to 1000 bats may gather in roofs, caves, attics, barns, churches, bridges or hollow trees.

Large groups of female bats often gather together in buildings to have their young.

In summer, **female** bats gather in groups to have their young. These groups are called **nursery roosts**. There may be hundreds of bat mothers in one place!

Bat young

This baby bat (front) with its mother is 10 days old. Its hair started to grow at four days old.

A **female** pipistrelle bat usually has one baby a year. When the baby is born it is about the size of a bumble bee. At first its eyes and ears are closed and it has no hair.

This baby pipistrelle bat is suckling from its mother.

Baby bats start to **suckle** right away. They drink milk from their mother's body. A baby bat clings tightly to its mother's furry belly when it feeds.

Growing up

Baby pipistrelle bats stay together in the nursery roost while their mothers go out to feed at night.

Baby bats soon crawl, but they cannot fly. At first, they stay in the **nursery roost**. Their mothers leave them somewhere safe while they go out to feed.

This young pipistrelle bat is ready to learn to fly.

When baby bats are three weeks old they learn to fly. They go out **hunting** with their mothers. By six weeks old they can find food for themselves.

Bat sounds

Most children can hear the chattering noises pipistrelle bats make when they call out to each other.

Bats use squeaks for **echolocation**. They make different sounds to tell each other things. They make a lot of chattering noises just before they go out to **hunt**.

Baby bats call out so their mothers can find them.

Baby bats in **nursery roosts** squeak loudly when their mothers return from hunting. Mothers recognize their own young from the sounds they make and by their smell.

Under attack

Owls hunt at night. They sometimes catch bats to eat.

Pipistrelle bats have many **predators**. Owls and **birds of prey** catch bats as they fly. Other predators, such as rats and cats, catch them on their **perch**.

This pipistrelle bat has squeezed into a tree to rest in the daytime. Predators cannot see it here!

Pipistrelle bats are small enough to squeeze into places where predators cannot see them. A pipistrelle bat is so tiny that with its wings folded, it could fit into a matchbox!

Dangers

Farmers sometimes need to cut down hedges and trees to make fields bigger.

Many farmers use sprays that kill **insects**. This means there are fewer insects for bats to eat. When people cut down hedges and trees, there are fewer places for bats to live.

Laws that protect bats say that if you have bats in your attic, you should leave them alone.

The number of pipistrelle bats in Britain has gone down in the last few years. Now there are **laws** to stop people from harming bats or the places where they live.

A bat's year

A young bat, like this, needs to eat a lot in summer so it can survive the winter.

Baby bats are usually born in summer. In summer there are lots of **insects** about. Young bats need to eat lots of insects to grow big and strong before winter comes.

This Daubenton's bat is sleeping out the winter in a coalmine.

In winter there are fewer insects for bats to eat. Some kinds of bats **hibernate**. They find somewhere safe from **predators** and the cold. They go into a deep sleep for the winter.

Bats in Britain

The pipistrelle is one kind of bat that lives in Britain. Here are some others. What differences can you see between these and the pipistrelle bat?

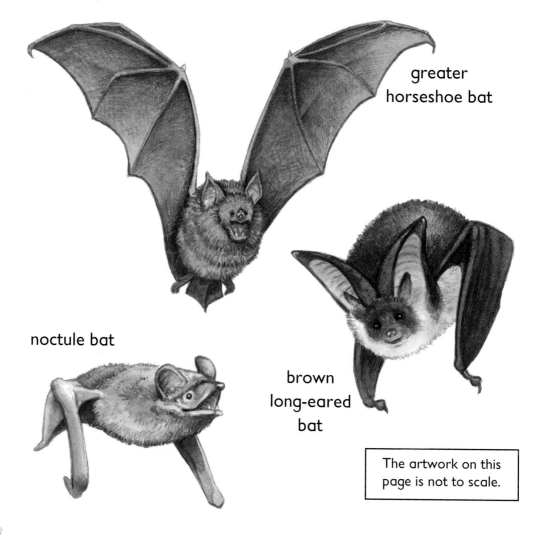

greater horseshoe bat

noctule bat

brown long-eared bat

The artwork on this page is not to scale.

Glossary

birds of prey large, strong birds that hunt and catch other animals for food

echo noise made when sounds bounce off objects

echolocation (say 'eko–lo–kay–shon') when an animal makes noises, then listens to the echoes to find its way around and to catch animals to eat

energy animals need energy to live and be active

female animal that can become a mother when it is grown up

hibernate when animals go into a very deep sleep over winter

hunt/hunting chasing and catching other animals in order to eat them

insect small animal that has six legs when an adult

law official rule of a country

mammals group of animals that feed babies on their own milk and have some hair on their bodies

marsh land that is soaked with water most of the time

nocturnal being active at night

nursery roost place where female bats gather to have and care for their young

perch place where bats and birds rest, such as a branch or roof

predator animal that catches and eats other animals for food

suckle when a mother feeds her baby with milk from her body. A baby bat sucks milk from teats on its mother's belly.

Index